Friction and Gravity
SNOWBOARDING SCIENCE

Marcus Figorito

The Rosen Publishing Group's
PowerKids Press™
New York

Published in 2009 by The Rosen Publishing Group, Inc.
29 East 21st Street, New York, NY 10010

Book Design: Haley W. Harasymiw

Photo Credits: Cover © Krzysxtof Tkacz/Shutterstock; p. 5 © Peter Gudella/Shutterstock; p. 7 © James Steidl/Shutterstock; p. 8 © Darko Novakovic/Shutterstock; p. 11 © Monkey Business Images/Shutterstock; p. 12 © David Stoecklein/Corbis; p. 14 (grab) © Purestock/Getty Images; p. 14 (grind) © Action Photos/Shutterstock; p. 17 © Eugen Shevchenko/Shutterstock; p. 18 © Olivier Renck/Aurora/Getty Images; p. 20 © Barbara Tripp/Shutterstock; p. 21 © igor ermakov/Shutterstock; p. 22 © Dubrovskiy Sergey Vladimirovic/ Shutterstock; p. 23 © Zhiltsov Alexandr/Shutterstock; p. 24 © Hirlesteanu Constantin-Ciprian/Shutterstock; p. 26 © Jeff Curtes/Corbis; p. 27 (parallel giant slalom) © Troy Wayrynen/ NewsSport/Corbis; p. 27 (snowboard cross) © Alexandra Winkler/Reuters/Corbis; p. 28 © AFP/Getty Images; p. 29 (Shannon Dunn) © Bongarts/Getty Images; p. 29 (Shaun White) © Doug Pensinger/Getty Images.

Library of Congress Cataloging-in-Publication Data

Figorito, Marcus.
 Friction and gravity : snowboarding science / Marcus Figorito.
      p. cm.
 Includes index.
 ISBN 978-1-4358-0185-1 (pbk.)
 6-pack ISBN: 978-1-4358-0186-8
 ISBN 978-1-4358-2995-4 (lib. bdg.)
 1. Friction—Juvenile literature. 2. Gravity—Juvenile literature. 3. Snowboarding—Juvenile literature. I. Title.
 QC197.F54 2009
 531'.1134-dc22

                              2008048391

Manufactured in the United States of America

Contents

Grab Your Board!

Imagine you're at the top of a steep, snowy slope. A thin, 4-foot (1.2-m) board is fastened to your feet. You slide forward and head downhill, gathering speed as you go. You're snowboarding!

Snowboarding hasn't been around as long as skiing, sledding, and skating. Since it was introduced, however, it's become one of the most popular winter activities. People like the challenge of trying to stay on their feet while sliding down a mountain at a high speed. Many people who live in places that are warm year-round travel to snowy mountains to feel the thrill of snowboarding down a steep slope.

Snowboarding isn't as easy as it may look. It requires balance, strength, and skill. How do snowboarders make it down the slope without falling down? You may be surprised to hear that science is involved! In fact, learning a bit about the science of snowboarding may help you become a better snowboarder. Let's take a look at the development of snowboards, the science that makes them work, and a few of the amazing tricks performed by the best snowboarders in the world.

Have you ever tried snowboarding?
Do you have any friends who snowboard?

A Short History of Snowboards

On December 25, 1965, in Muskegon, Michigan, Sherman Poppen was watching his daughter playing outside. She was standing on her sled trying to keep her balance while sliding down a hill. This gave Poppen an idea that would soon change winter sports.

The First Board

Poppen went to his shed. He tied two skis together and fixed a rope to the front for the rider to hold. Poppen's wife, Nancy, called his invention the "Snurfer" because it let the rider surf in the snow. Soon other kids wanted Poppen to make them Snurfers, too. Poppen began to bind old water skies together to make Snurfers. Then he cut grooves into the bottom so the board would move better while going downhill. Finally, he put a metal edge around the board since the wooden edge wore down quickly.

Soon, Snurfers were in such demand that Poppen couldn't keep up. He sold his ideas to a business so that more Snurfers could be made. In

One type of binding allows the rider to click their boots into place when they step onto the board.

1966, about a half million Snurfers were sold. In the 1970s, Poppen helped start Snurfing competitions.

Soon other people were making their own kinds of Snurfers, some without rope. Jake Burton Carpenter entered one of the Snurfing competitions with his own special board. It had **bindings** that secured his feet to the board

tail

bindings

edge

base

nose

The smooth base on this snowboard
helps the rider move at a high speed
down a slope.

and gave him greater control over the direction and speed of the board. He later started a successful snowboard company.

Modern Snowboards

Just as Poppen made the first Snurfer in his shed, many early snowboards were homemade. Some resembled surfboards. Others resembled skateboards without wheels. Today, many different materials are used to make snowboards. Most snowboards are wood surrounded by layers of **fiberglass**. The bottom, or base, is usually plastic with a strip of steel around the edge. Snowboards must have a very smooth base with front and back ends—also called the nose and tail—that curve up slightly so the board can slide smoothly over the snow. Bindings fasten the rider's feet to the board.

Standard snowboards are usually 55 to 65 inches (140 to 165 cm) long and 9.5 to 11 inches (24 to 28 cm) wide. Children's snowboards are smaller. Different-shaped snowboards are used for different kinds of riding. For example, long, narrow racing—or alpine—snowboards are used for speed on long mountain courses. Shorter, wider park—or jib—snowboards provide more control and are used for performing tricks on shorter hills. Modern snowboards must be sturdy, light, and bendable.

What Makes You Go Down the Slope?

We know that the materials and shapes of snowboards help riders make it downhill successfully. However, the best-made snowboard on Earth wouldn't go anywhere without gravity.

What Is Gravity?

Gravity is the force that makes objects we drop fall to the ground. Because of gravity, all objects in the universe are attracted to each other. The greater an object's mass, the greater its force of gravity. The sun's gravity attracts Earth and causes Earth to travel around it. Earth's gravity attracts us, keeping us on the ground until another force overcomes it. For example, every time you take a step or jump in the air, you're using a force just a little greater than gravity to leave the ground.

Gravity is always pulling down on you with the same amount of force. It gives you and every object on Earth weight. When you're on flat ground, gravity keeps you in place. On level ground high in the mountains,

What will happen when the rider gets to the bottom of the hill? How will gravity affect her?

Even a small bump can help riders get their
snowboards high into the air.

gravity keeps snowboarders in place. When they move onto a slope, gravity pulls them downhill.

Defying Gravity

Have you ever heard the phrase "defying gravity"? This means moving or acting in a way that appears to defy, or act against, the force of gravity. Snowboarders can seem like they're defying gravity when they do amazing **stunts**. Instead, they're overcoming it for a few seconds before gravity brings them down again. Without gravity, they would just float away!

To get "air time," riders use large bumps on the slope or man-made **ski jumps**. As soon as their front foot passes over the bump's peak, the rider jumps. The faster their speed, the higher they'll get. They have only a short time in the air to perform a trick. Let's take a look at some of the amazing tricks snowboarders can do before gravity brings them down again.

THAT KID IS GOOFY!

You may hear people say snowboarders are "regular" or "goofy." This has nothing to do with their personalities. These words refer to the snowboarder's style of riding. In a regular stance, or the way a rider stands on their board, the left foot is closest to the nose of the snowboard. In a goofy stance, the right foot is closest to the nose. Both stances are common. Experienced snowboarders ride both regular and goofy.

Snowboarding Tricks

Spins and flips are tricks snowboarders perform in the air. Some are measured in degrees. To better understand degrees, picture yourself standing in the middle of a giant clock, looking at the 12 o'clock position. You perform a 90-degree **rotation** by turning to face the 3 o'clock position, which is a quarter of a circle. A 180-degree rotation means turning halfway around the circle to face 6 o'clock. A 270-degree rotation is turning to 9 o'clock, or three-quarters of

Spins and flips are just two kinds of tricks. Other tricks involve sliding the board on a rail (grind) and grabbing the snowboard in midair (grab).

grind

grab

the way around. A 360-degree rotation is turning completely around. Sometimes snowboarders rotate themselves in the air more than once! Each quarter turn adds another 90 degrees and more difficulty to the trick.

AIR TRICKS

ollie—The rider jumps off the tail of their board and into the air.

nollie—The rider jumps off the nose of their board and into the air.

SPINS

shifty—The rider twists their hips to rotate 90 degrees and then brings the board back to the original position.

bs air (backside)—This is a clockwise spin for regular riders and a counterclockwise spin for goofy riders.

fs air (frontside)—This is a counterclockwise spin for regular riders and a clockwise spin for goofy riders.

FLIPS

backflip—The rider flips backward off a jump.

front flip—The rider flips forward off a jump

mctwist—The rider moves forward, rotates 540 degrees in a backside direction while performing a front flip, and lands riding forward.

Riders have invented many more tricks. After performing any stunt, snowboarders need to position their board so it lands flat on the ground. If they don't, they may break their board or hurt themselves.

Riding with Friction

Another force helps snowboarders ride, control, and eventually stop at the bottom of the hill. Just as important as gravity is the force of **friction**.

Overcoming Friction

Friction occurs when two surfaces rub against each other. The more friction there is, the harder it is to slide. For example, friction between a car's tires and the road helps the car stay on the road. Snow and ice reduce friction on a road, causing cars to slide.

Friction prevents snowboarders from sliding down a hill covered with grass, dirt, or rocks. A snowboarding slope needs to be **slippery** and smooth for the snowboard to slide well. Snow and ice on the slope help, but the base of the snowboard has to be smooth as well. People sometimes wax the bottom of their snowboards to make them even more slippery. The less friction there is between the board and the slope, the faster the snowboarder can go.

When a snowboarder stands at the top of a slope, there is a lot of friction between the board and the ground. To overcome this

Did you know that friction occurs between the snowboarder and air? It's true! The friction between the air and your body slows you as you slide down a slope.

Some snowboarders also like to sandboard!
Sandboarders rub wax on the bottom of
their board. This reduces the friction between the
board and the sand.

friction, the snowboarder must use force to move. This is similar to the force we use to overcome gravity when we jump. Once the board starts to move, another aspect of friction actually helps its movement—heat.

A Slippery Slope

Friction between two objects creates heat. Rub your hands together. The harder you rub, the warmer your hands get. The same thing happens between a snowboard and snow. The friction created as a snowboard slides over snow generates heat that melts the snow, resulting in a thin layer of water between the board and the snow. This water works as **lubrication**, making the slope more slippery. Just as people use oil to reduce friction between machine parts, water

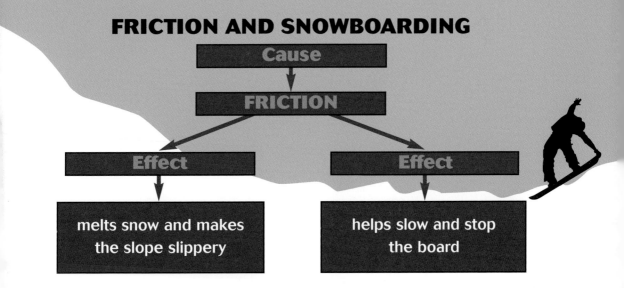

FRICTION AND SNOWBOARDING

Cause

FRICTION

Effect

Effect

melts snow and makes the slope slippery

helps slow and stop the board

reduces friction between the board and the snow, allowing the board to slide more easily.

As the ground levels at the bottom of the slope, the effect of gravity lessens and the effect of friction increases, bringing the board to a stop.

Carving

Friction also helps the snowboarder "carve," or make quick turns, on the way down the mountain. To turn, the snowboarder leans to the left or right, aiming into the turn. Leaning tips the snowboard onto its hard metal edge. The edge doesn't slide over the slope as the bottom does. It digs into it, much like a

You can see how this snowboarder handles a steep slope, carving sharp turns to keep control of the board.

knife carves food. Enough friction is produced to turn the board, but the metal edge is smooth enough to prevent the board from slowing too much. It's actually easier to carve when traveling at a fast speed. Carving is also used to keep the board from going too fast down a hill and causing the rider to lose control. When the board digs into the slope, it throws snow away from the snowboarder.

Sideslips

To make a quick stop, the snowboarder quickly turns the board **perpendicular** to the hill, or 180 degrees. This is called a sideslip. The edge of the board digs deep into the slope, like the blade of a snowplow. The board creates so much friction that it stops abruptly.

How Do I Stop Falling Down?

When learning to snowboard, new riders spend much of their time falling down. How can you avoid this? Don't stand up straight!

You can see in many pictures that experienced snowboarders don't stand up straight on their way down a hill. If they did this, they would fall down almost immediately. In fact, riders need to constantly lean left or right. They lean to balance the different forces at work on the slope.

The Center of Gravity

Snowboarders must work to keep their **center of gravity** properly positioned as they go down a slope. The center of gravity is the point on an object—or a person—where weight seems to be **concentrated**. For an object or a person to be balanced, the pull of gravity must be the same on all its parts. For example, if you lean over too far in your chair, your center of gravity will move too far to the side and cause you

A snowboarder's center of gravity must be over the edge of the snowboard that's in contact with the snow.

to fall. If you sit up straight, all your weight is concentrated in the middle, helping you balance.

Balancing

A snowboarder must constantly shift their center of gravity to stay upright on their moving board. If they don't, they'll fall. Maintaining the proper

What would happen if this snowboarder leaned too far forward or backward?

position can be difficult depending on the angle of the slope. Many new snowboarders want to lean back when they start down a hill. Instead, they should lean forward to balance the force pushing them back. This is the only way to be in the right position to carve, stop, and adjust your speed.

Riders need to lean when they carve. Leaning balances a snowboarder's weight against the force of the turn. When these are equal, the rider won't fall. After the turn, the snowboarder moves their weight and returns the board flat to the ground.

Keeping their knees bent also helps a rider keep control. Being closer to the ground helps them maintain their balance. The lower an object's center of gravity, the less likely it is to fall over.

Playing with Gravity?

You've seen the center of gravity at work in many situations. On a playground seesaw, for example, the center of gravity is in the middle when no one is on either end. When children of different weights sit on each side, the center of gravity changes toward the heavier child. The heavier child needs to move toward the middle to make the center of gravity shift to the middle again.

Olympic Snowboarding

Snowboarding competitions have become very popular. Snowboarders love to show off their talents, and fans love to see them "defy gravity." In 1998, snowboarding became an Olympic sport, which is one of the highest honors a sport can receive. Since 2006, men and women compete in three Olympic events.

halfpipe

Halfpipe

The halfpipe is a trench shaped liked the letter "U," or like a pipe cut in half lengthwise. Snowboarders go up and down the sides of the trench to pick up speed. They can launch off the top of a side and do different tricks. Judges score the tricks based on difficulty and completion.

event	course	race	obstacles	jumps	tricks
halfpipe					✔
parallel giant slalom	✔	✔	✔		
snowboard cross	✔	✔	✔	✔	

parallel giant slalom

Parallel Giant Slalom

A slalom is a downhill race in which the rider follows a zigzag course marked by flags. In parallel giant slalom, two identical courses are set up side by side, and athletes race to the bottom. A rider who goes off course loses.

Snowboard Cross

In snowboard cross, four riders race through **obstacles** and over jumps before reaching the finish line. They often crash into each other.

snowboard cross

In all three of these events, the forces of gravity and friction allow the snowboarders to reach high speeds, control their boards, and stop to get their medals!

Some Famous Snowboarders

The popularity of snowboarding has grown quickly since the 1960s. People all over the world appreciate the talent of the best snowboarders and are inspired to acquire the skills to master their tricks. Let's take a look at some famous snowboarders who have helped bring snowboarding into the spotlight.

Terje Haakonsen

Norwegian Terje Haakonsen has been called the "Michael Jordan" of snowboarding because he excels at the sport, especially halfpipe, and has won most of the competitions he's been in. He invented a very difficult trick in which the rider flips 720 degrees! It's called the Haakon flip.

Terje Haakonsen has been the subject of several films.

Shannon Dunn-Downing

Shannon Dunn-Downing, a halfpipe champion, was the first woman to complete several difficult tricks in competition. At the 1998 Olympics in Nagano, Japan, she became the first American woman to win a snowboarding medal. Since then, she has worked to encourage more women to snowboard.

Shaun White

American Shaun White is sometimes called the "Flying Tomato" because of his red hair and his ability to jump high into the air. He won a gold medal at the 2006 Olympics in Torino, Italy, for halfpipe and has many **X-Games** medals as well. Shaun is so popular that he has a snowboarding video game named after him.

Hit the Slopes!

Learning to snowboard takes patience. Knowing how to lean and balance is a skill that can be mastered through practice. In time—and perhaps after falling down many times—you will improve. This winter, you may find yourself "catching some air"! Luckily, you have friction and gravity to help you safely reach the bottom of the slope.

Take a look below and start practicing another skill on the slopes—the special language of snowboarding!

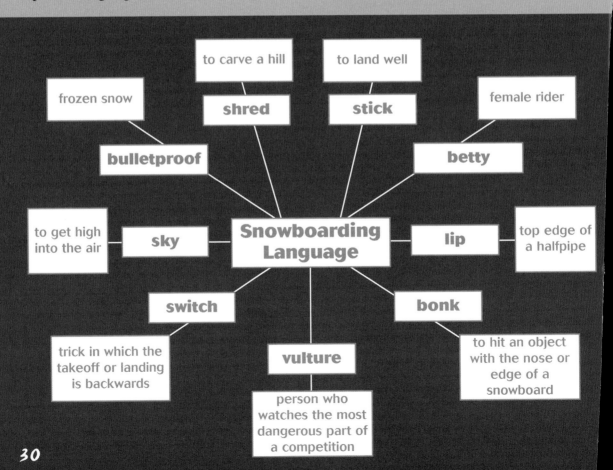

Glossary

binding (BYN-ding) Something used to secure your boots onto a snowboard.

center of gravity (SEHN-tuhr UV GRA-vuh-tee) The point where an object's weight seems to be concentrated.

concentrate (KAHN-suhn-trayt) To gather into one place.

fiberglass (FY-buhr-glas) A strong material made of pressed glass fibers.

friction (FRIHK-shun) A force that resists motion between two things in contact.

lubrication (loo-bruh-KAY-shun) Something that reduces friction between two objects.

obstacle (AHB-stuh-kuhl) Something that is in the way.

perpendicular (puhr-puhn-DIH-kyuh-luhr) Having to do with two lines that cross to form right, or 90-degree, angles.

rotation (roh-TAY-shun) The act or process of spinning in a circle around a center point.

ski jump (SKEE JUMP) A steep, man-made slope with a sharp upturn at the bottom.

slippery (SLIH-puh-ree) Causing something to slide easily.

stunt (STUNT) An act that needs special skills or strength to do.

X Games (EHKS GAYMZ) An annual event involving dangerous sports where athletes from around the world compete against one another to determine who is the best in their sport.

Index